Angels: God's Servants For You

Keith A. Butler Sr.

Unless otherwise indicated, all Scripture quotations in this volume are from the *King James Version* of the Bible.

Third Printing 2001

ISBN 1-893575-07-1

Word of Faith Publishing
20000 W. Nine Mile Road
Southfield, MI 48075-5597

Contents

Contents

Chapter 1

Angels Have a Purpose!

I'm going to share with you on the subject of angels, God's servants *for* you, because I am going to show you from God's Word that one of God's purposes for angels is service for you, the believer.

The purpose in my writing this book is to help you to understand the ministry of angels — how it operates — and to teach you how you can cause your angel to be able to do his job better!

As a believer, you have available to you the ministry of angels.

> **HEBREWS 1:13,14**
> **13 But to which of the angels said he** [God] **at any time, Sit on my right hand, until I make thine enemies thy footstool?**
> **14 Are they** [angels] **not all ministering spirits, sent forth to minister FOR them who shall be heirs** [or recipients] **of salvation?**

Now if you don't have that word "for" underlined in your Bible, underline it, because the word "for" carries a different meaning than the word "to," as in "minister *to* them...." Angels have a purpose, and their purpose is service *for* you, the believer, an heir of salvation.

Read carefully the following passage of Scripture concerning angels.

> **HEBREWS 2:1-7**
> **1 Therefore we ought to give the more earnest heed to the things which we have heard, lest at any time we should let them slip** [or "let them leak out"]**.**
> **2 For if the word spoken by angels was stedfast, and every transgression and disobedience received a just recompence of reward;**
> **3 How shall we escape, if we neglect so great salvation; which at the first began to be spoken by the Lord, and was confirmed unto us by them that heard him;**
> **4 God also bearing them witness, both with signs and wonders, and with divers miracles, and gifts of the Holy Ghost, according to his own will?**
> **5 For unto the angels hath he not put in subjection the world to come, whereof we speak.**
> **6 But one in a certain place testified, saying, What is man, that thou art mindful of him? or the son of man, that thou visitest him?**
> **7 Thou madest him a little lower than the angels; thou crownedst him with glory and honour, and didst set him over the works of thy hands:**

One of the things that the Church needs to have restoration of is the ministry of angels. Yes, prosperity should be restored to the Church; we as believers should receive our money back that the devil has stolen from us because of a lack of knowledge.

And *healing* ought to be restored to the Church — and we should have our family relationships restored too. We should receive and walk in *everything* God has for us, including the ministry of angels that God provided for the Old Testament and New Testament saints.

We can read about the ministry of angels throughout the Word of God. We can read that the saints of God, even as late as in the Book of Acts, had a very high understanding of the ministry of angels. And angels operated in their lives because those men and women of God *expected* them to operate and did what God said to do to release the ministry of angels on their behalf.

There hasn't been a lot of teaching on angels in the Body of Christ, but I'm going to give you quite a bit in this book. I didn't say I'm going to give you every word on the subject, but I'm going to share with you what I've learned. It's vitally important that Christians everywhere learn that angels are God's servants *for* us.

A Heavenly Ministration

Remember Hebrews 1:14 says, *"Are they* [angels] *not ALL ministering spirits, sent forth to minister for them who shall be heirs of salvation?"* "All" means *every one of them*. Every angel of God is a ministering spirit. You see angels are not just spirits; they're *ministering* spirits. Their job is to minister to anyone who is an heir of salvation. The word "minister" means *to assist; to aid;* and *to help*.

Hebrews 1:14 also says that angels are "sent forth," which means they are *anointed*. So we could say that the angels have been anointed to assist, to aid, and to help anyone who is an heir of salvation! (If you are a Christian, you are an heir of salvation.)

Ten Ways Angels Are Involved
In Our Lives

In God's Word, I have found instances of angels doing ten different things regarding the children of God. I'm going to give them to you up front, in no particular order. Then we'll go through the Scriptures and study each one in more detail.

Number *one*, we find in the Word of God that angels are involved in *healing*. Number *two*, angels are involved in *delivering*.

Three, angels are involved in *strengthening*. The Greek word translated "strengthening" means *invigorating*!

Number *four*, angels are involved in *giving revelation from God*. Number *five*, they are talked about in the Word of God as *doing battle*!

Six, there is an instance of angels *handling the death of Christians*. Number *seven*, angels are involved in *protecting believers*. Number *eight*, they are described as *looking just like us* — so much so that we can't tell the difference between an angel and a human being!

Number *nine*, angels are involved in *delivering messages* — even to Jesus Himself. And, *ten*, we find in the Word angels *leading the way into the future* for the children of God.

That's a pretty impressive list! Even in the New Testament, angels are involved in all the things I've just mentioned. God intended for angels to minister to — to assist, aid, and help — anyone who is an heir of salvation!

Hebrews 2:3 says, *"How shall we escape, if we neglect so great salvation. . . ?"* In other words, how shall we walk in total victory if we don't have the ministry of angels working for us the way God intended it to work?

Many don't realize the role of angels in our everyday lives, but angels are always with us. If the gift of discerning of spirits (1 Cor. 12:10) were in operation, you would be able to see in the spirit realm the angels who are always with you.

Incidentally, this spiritual gift is called discerning of spirits, *not* the gift of discernment. I've heard people say, "Well, I have the gift of discernment, and I can tell whether people are good or bad."

No, they don't have the gift of discernment. What they have is a gift of *suspicion*!

In First Corinthians chapter 12, the Apostle Paul lists the revelation gifts — the word of wisdom, word of knowledge, and discerning of spirits. The word "discern" means *to see.* So when the gift of discerning of spirits is in operation, a person can *see* into the realm of the spirit.

If you had an manifestation of discerning of spirits right now, you would see that the room you are in is full of angels. Standing by your seat or by your side are your angels. And I would say that many of them are dormant. That simply means they are not active to the full extent that God intended. (I'll talk more about that in the next chapter.)

God intended for angels to minister to you — to assist, aid, and help you — throughout your entire life and in every area of your life.

Angels Excel in Strength

First, I want you to notice that one of the characteristics of angels is that they are super strong! Psalm 103:20 says that they excel in strength! In other words, they are *strong, strong, strong*! That is the reason why one of them, after looking at man, asked the Lord, "Now, what is man that You are mindful of them?" (Heb. 2:6).

In today's language, the angel mentioned in Hebrews 2:6 was probably saying, "Mankind is puny. They're *weak*. God, what is it about them that You are mindful of them and that You spend so much time visiting them instead of us!"

You Are More Precious Than Angels!

Hebrews 2:6 is telling us that we are more precious to God than the angels: "... *What is man, that thou art mindful of him? or the son of man, that thou visitest him?*"

It's as if the angels are saying, "Men can't do what we do! Men can't knock down the walls of Jericho! One man can't take care of an entire Egyptian army, but one angel can! So what is man, God, that You are so mindful of them? You're spending all your time thinking about *them*! What's up? We're the 'bad' ones — we're the tough ones! Look at how frail they are, God. Why are You giving them all the attention instead of us?"

I'll tell you why God is so mindful of you. Because, in His sight, you are more precious than angels!

Let's read again in Hebrews chapter 2.

> **HEBREWS 2:5**
> 5 For unto the angels hath he [God] **not put in subjection the world to come, whereof we speak.**

The writer said in this verse that the angels will not have the world to come — the world of the future — in subjection.

Did you know that there is a future world coming? The current world is going to pass away, and there's going to be a new heaven and a new earth (Rev. 21:1). But the angels aren't going to be the ones that are going to be the "bad boys"! They're not going to be the ones in charge.

No, First Corinthians 6 says that *we* shall judge the angels, and *we* shall rule" (v. 3).

HEBREWS 2:6
6 But one [angel] **in a certain place testified, saying, What is man, that thou art mindful of him? or the son of man, that thou visitest him?**

Now that you understand how strong an angel is, I hope you can appreciate the angel's remarks. When he asks, "What is man?" You see, angels are watching to see what God does with "dirt-bags" like us!

I mean, I can just imagine Michael the archangel seated near the throne of God, carrying out all God's assignments. Michael is the greatest angel in Heaven! And God says, "Michael, you're My man! You're good! But move over. I have some-one I'm going to give a higher place to."

Michael says, "Well, whoever that is must be pretty 'bad'!" Then God introduces *you*! And Michael says, *"What!"*

That's why in verse 6, an angel asked, "God, what is man? All You do is think about *him*."

Did you know that all God does is think about you — about how He's going to bless, help, and deliver you, meet your needs, and keep you safe?

Don't you tell me God doesn't love you! The angel testified about man, "You're always thinking about him! And You're always visiting him!"

Can you just hear Michael saying, "You don't spend time with *me*, God. I kill armies for You. I deliver Your people. And You don't even visit me. You're down there with those 'dirt-bags.'"

HEBREWS 2:7
7 Thou madest him [man] a little lower than the angels; thou CROWNEDST him with GLORY and honour, and didst set him over the works of thy hands.

Do you know what the glory of God is? It's the Holy Spirit, the anointing!

I can just hear God saying to the angels, "Don't call them dirt-bags again, because they are My sons and daughters. I'm going to crown them with glory and honor."

HEBREWS 2:8
8 Thou hast put ALL THINGS IN SUBJECTION under his feet. For in that he put all in subjection under him, he left NOTHING THAT IS NOT PUT UNDER HIM. But now we see not yet all things put under him.

What does this verse mean? It means that all things are supposed to be under your feet! And before Jesus comes, He's going to have a Church that's just like that. Everything will be restored to what was God's original intent! We are to reign in life by Jesus Christ (Rom. 5:17).

HEBREWS 2:9
9 But we see JESUS, who was MADE a little lower than the angels for the suffering of death, crowned with glory and honour; that he by the grace of God should taste death for every man.

We know from reading verse 7 that man was made a little lower than the angels. But how was *Jesus* made a little lower than the angels? He was made a "dirt-bag" like me and you! God, who created the world, left the royal diadem in glory and came and wrapped Himself in dirt-bag flesh so that He could taste death for you and me!

Jesus died on the Cross and carried our sins so that we could cease being dirt-bags and cease being doomed to hell. Jesus became flesh so that we could have our sins paid for and so that God could elevate us over the angel and make us his boss! We will judge angels, because we are heirs of salvation. Angels are God's servants for us.

> **HEBREWS 2:!0,11**
> **10 For it became him** [Jesus], **for whom are all things, and by whom are all things, in bringing many sons unto glory, to make the captain of their salvation perfect through sufferings.**
> **11 For both he** [Jesus] **that sanctifieth and they who are sanctified** [man] **are all of one: for which cause he is not ashamed to call them** [man] **brethren,**

The word "sanctified" means *one who is set apart.* We have been set apart because of Jesus. Sanctification is not whether or not women put on make-up. And sanctification is not wearing a dress that drags to the floor!

No, sanctification is whether or not you have received Jesus! He said, *"...BOTH he that sanctifieth and they who are sanctified ARE ALL OF ONE...."* There is no difference in the sight of God!

We Are in Union With Christ

Jesus is the Son of God. And because of Jesus, *you* are a son or daughter of God if you have accepted Him as Savior. God the Father doesn't love Jesus any more than He loves you. And all that He gave Jesus, He gave to you! In other words, He made us one with Him.

The rest of verse 11 says, *"...for which cause he is not ashamed to call them brethren."* In other words, the "dirt-bags" — *us* — turned out to be the ones seated at the table with Jesus! Jesus, seated at the right hand of the throne of God, says to every believer, "Come on and sit down. You're My brother."

God loves you so much. You simply cannot understand with your mind or human intellect how great the salvation was that He provided for you. I don't understand how people can turn their back on God and backslide after all He's done for them. If they really understood it, they wouldn't say, "I don't want to live for You anymore. I just want to do things *my* way."

Your Protector — Your Angel — Is Also Your Servant

Yet many do just that. Angels have been protecting these people their entire life, but they turn away from God and from what He has provided for them.

God took your protectors — angels — and made them your servants! He's provided for you such a great salvation, so serve Him with gladness, not sadness. And don't turn your back on Him.

First Peter chapter 1 gives us some more insight as to the place we have with God.

> **1 PETER 1:10-12**
> **10 Of which salvation the prophets have enquired and searched diligently, who prophesied of the grace that should come unto you:**
> **11 Searching what, or what manner of time the Spirit of Christ which was in them did signify, when it testified beforehand the sufferings of Christ, and the glory that should follow.**
> **12 Unto whom it was revealed, that not unto themselves, but unto us they did minister the things, which are now reported unto you by them that have preached the gospel unto you with the Holy Ghost sent down from heaven; which things the angels desire to look into.**

In verses 10 and 11, Peter is talking about Old Testament prophets who received all that revelation, but it wasn't even for them; it was for you and me.

Then verse 12 says, "*. . . which things the angels desire to look into.*" You see, the angels see us singing songs of deliverance unto God. The angels look into that, but they can't sing those songs of deliverance. They can't sing songs of salvation. They can't sing songs of mercy and grace and blessing.

Why not? Because there is no mercy to an angel. Those angels that disobeyed God once — Satan and a third of the angels that followed him — were banned forever and will be damned forever. They were banned over one transgression.

Yet how many times have *you and I* transgressed? How many times have *we* not obeyed God? Yet God hasn't said, "One time you missed it; now be damned forever!"

No! God said, "You missed it. Now come to Me, and I'll help you and give you another chance." And He's done it again and again and again!

You Are Special — Set Apart From All of God's Creation

God loves you! You are special! You see, regardless of how beautiful the planets, the universe, the trees and flowers, and the angels are, none of these things means anything to God compared to what you and I mean to Him. There's only one thing that God created that really means anything to Him, and that is *us*! We're the only thing that matters to God. Everything else does not even come close to second!

So how can we dare say, "It's not God's will for me to be blessed. It's God's will for me to be impoverished. It's God's will for me to be sick"? Anyone who says those things doesn't understand Hebrews 1 and 2.

God loves you so much. There's only one reason why He created the planets, the universe, the flowers, the trees, the gold, the silver, and everything else He's made. That reason was *to give it to you*!

Why? Because you're His child. Certainly, we were born in sin, but God said, "If they will receive the One who paid the price for their sin, I will adopt them into My family and forget they ever had a past. I will treat them as though sin never existed in their life."

I once ministered this message, and the Lord gave me the following psalm:

> The angels of God were sent to you
>
> To help you through and through,
>
> To help you navigate the way in whatever the enemy brings against you today.
>
> So go before God, worship and praise Him, and speak His words,
>
> And, yea, watch Him do what He said.
>
> For He shall send His angel before thee to clear the way,

And the enemy shall not be able to stop you this or any other day.

For the angel is strong, don't you see?

And he has been sent to deliver thee.

Yea, he was sent for *you*, yes, for you, don't you see?

To be the one to deliver those who have received the King of kings.

Thank God for the ministry of angels. Yes, Jesus was made so much better. But because of Him, *you* were made so much better too. Angels are God's servants *for* you. So determine to receive and benefit from the ministry of angels that God has provided.

Chapter 2

How To 'Activate' The Angels

Angels are our servants. We could say that angels are, for lack of a better term, "robots." In effect, they have been programmed, and the only thing they can do is what they have been programmed to do. If we push their "on" button, they operate. If we push their "off" button, they stop operating. We can turn that button on, and we can turn that button off.

Your Angel Can Be Active Or Dormant in Your Life

In other words, before we can have the ministry of angels working in our lives, we must first understand what it is that causes angels to be "activated." I use the word "activated" because angels can remain dormant. Although angels are always with us, they can remain dormant and never even begin to operate and minister for us as God intended.

How do you activate the ministry of angels on your behalf? The answer is found in Psalm 103.

PSALM 103:20
20 Bless the Lord, ye his angels, that excel in strength, that do his commandments, HEARKEN-ING UNTO THE VOICE OF HIS WORD.

We understand from this verse of Scripture that angels hearken unto the commands of the Lord — unto God's Word. Angels still do this today. God gives angels their instructions, and they listen and obey.

That also means that when *we* say what God's Word says — when we speak God's Word — we loose or release angels to work on our behalf. But when we speak words *contrary* to what God has said, we bind or hinder our angels from working for us.

How To Speak With the 'Voice of God'

It is important for us to know that angels hear-ken unto the voice of God. It is also important to know how God's voice is manifested. God's voice is not only manifested by God's speaking from His throne or through the Holy Ghost — the voice of

God is manifested when *believers* speak in line with His Word!

When we speak God's Word, we are speaking with the "voice of God"!

You see, the Bible is God speaking to you and me. And God said in Isaiah 55:11 that His Word will not return to Him void. In other words, when the Word of God is spoken out of the mouth of a believer, it is the same as God the Father speaking it, and the angels hearken unto God's Word spoken by a believer the same way they do when God Himself gives a command from His throne!

We can command our angels to minister for us by speaking on the authority of God's Word.

You Can Loose Your Angels!

I want you to see something in Matthew chapter 18 concerning the ministry of angels. In this particular passage, Jesus is talking. These words may be very familiar to you, but I want you to see them in a new light.

MATTHEW 18:18
18 Verily [or, "Truly" or, "I'm not lying about this" or, "This is the truth I'm telling you"!] **I say unto you, Whatsoever ye shall bind on earth shall be bound**

> **in heaven: and whatsoever ye shall LOOSE on
> earth shall be LOOSED in heaven.**

Many Christians talk about *binding* things, especially demons, with their words, but Matthew 18:18 also says that whatever you *loose* on earth will also be loosed in the heavenlies.

The "heaven" or heavenlies in this verse that Jesus is referring to is not the third Heaven where God dwells. And it's not the stellar heaven, which we call outer space. No, it's the atmospheric heaven that's all around this earth. The atmosphere around this earth is where all the "fighting" is taking place. The winner is determined by what you bind or loose with the words of your mouth.

So we see from this verse that whatever you bind is *bound*. But we also see that whatever you loose is *loosed*! This verse is not just talking about binding demons. You can *loose* your angels! And you loose your angels the same way you bind demons — with the words of your mouth coming in line with God's Word.

You see, God has given us the "tree of life," and it's in our mouth. Proverbs 18:21 says that death and life are in the power of the tongue. Your words not only *produce* things, they also *bind* demon spirits and *loose* the ministry of angels!

You can talk to your angel and tell your angel what his assignment will be just as you can make a demand on anything else that God has provided to help you. So binding and loosing is in operation concerning the ministry of angels. With the words of your mouth, you can loose your angel to operate on your behalf, or you can bind or hinder him by speaking the wrong words. That means you'd better start paying attention to what you're saying!

EPHESIANS 4:29
29 Let no corrupt communication proceed out of your mouth, but that which is good to the use of edifying, that it may minister grace unto the hearers.

Notice that in this verse, corrupt communication is not defined as cursing. Corrupt communication is defined as *anything that is not edifying*. Whatever doesn't build you up personally and doesn't build anyone else up is considered corrupt communication. In other words, corrupt communication doesn't just apply to talking negatively about someone else; it is also applies to the words you speak over your own life.

When you say things, such as, "I can't make it," "I can't do it," "I don't know what I'm going to do," or "Everyone is against me" you are involved in corrupt communication. Or if you say, "I'm too

young to be a success" or "I'm too old to do anything for God," that is corrupt communication.
Those words don't line up with God's Word,
because with God, all things are possible (Mark
10:27)!

When a believer is agreeing with God's Word,
such as Mark 10:27, which says, ". . .*with God all
things are possible,*" he will have angels helping
him and doing things for him! That believer will
have angels bringing him money and doing all ten
of the things that angels are mentioned as doing in
the Word of God. He will have angels delivering messages. He will have angels delivering people from
bondage. He will have angels doing some of everything!

Corrupt Communication Will Bind Angels and Hinder Your Blessing

Let's look again at Ephesians chapter 4.

EPHESIANS 4:29,30
**29 Let no corrupt communication proceed out of
your mouth, but that which is good to the use of edifying, that it may minister grace unto the hearers.
30 And grieve not the holy Spirit of God, whereby ye
are sealed unto the day of redemption.**

If a believer can grieve the Spirit of God through corrupt communication, then he can also through corrupt communication stop what the angels of God were sent to do for him.

The words that come out of our mouth are extremely important. What we say and how we say it has a whole lot to do with what happens in our life. What we say and how we say it also applies to how to talk to others.

Entertaining Angels 'Unawares'

I'm going to show you from God's Word the importance of how we talk to others.

> **HEBREWS 13:1,2**
> 1 Let brotherly love continue.
> 2 Be not forgetful to entertain strangers: for thereby some have entertained angels UNAWARES [meaning they didn't even know it!].

Verse 2 ought to tell us something about the nature of angels. If we can look at an angel and not know it's an angel, then an angel must be able to take human form. As I said, angels are involved in looking just like us.

That means that someone you have met and talked to at one time in your life — someone who may have assisted you in some way — could have been an angel who came to you in human form. Perhaps it was necessary to get a word or a message to you.

Maybe someone in your church has come to you and told you something that was a revelation to you. You had never seen that person before and you've never seen him since that encounter. Well, that "person" may not have been a human being! He may have been an angel of God! (Maybe the one you got mad at because he took your seat at church was an angel sent by God to give you a word from Him — and you got mad at the angel!)

Hebrews 13:2 says, "Some people have entertained angels, and they didn't know they were angels." So the writer tells us in verse 1 to walk in love. Notice how the two verses of Scripture are connected. He says, "Walk in love, because some people have entertained angels and weren't aware of the fact."

In other words, we never know who we're dealing with, so we'd better walk in love with everyone we meet. We might be talking to the very one God sent to help us through a particular problem!

Don't Provoke Your Angel!

I'm going to show you in the Word of God that we can go against our angel and actually provoke him. In provoking our angel, we can prevent him from doing what God intended for him to do for us.

Now remember what we read in our golden text: *"... the word spoken by angels was stedfast, and every transgression and disobedience received a just recompense of reward"* (Heb. 2:2).

In other words, the man who received a word from an angel of God also received a just reward based on what his response to that word was. Whether or not he believed what the angel said and whether or not he then spoke words of belief or unbelief determined his reward.

Let me show you an example of a man in the Bible who provoked an angel.

LUKE 1:5, 9-13
5 There was in the days of Herod, the king of Judaea, a certain priest named Zacharias, of the course of Abia: and his wife was of the daughters of Aaron, and her name was Elisabeth....
9 According to the custom of the priest's office, his lot was to burn incense when he went into the temple of the Lord.
10 And the whole multitude of the people were praying without at the time of incense.

> **11 And there appeared unto him an ANGEL of the
> Lord standing on the right side of the altar of
> incense.
> 12 And when Zacharias saw him, he was troubled,
> and fear fell upon him.
> 13 But the angel said unto him, Fear not,
> Zacharias ...**

Now this angel came to deliver a message to
Zacharias. The angel was going to give him revelation about God's will concerning the future, which
is called a word of wisdom.

> **LUKE 1:13
> 13 But the angel said unto him, Fear not,
> Zacharias thy prayer is heard: and thy wife Elisa-
> beth shall bear thee a son, and thou shalt call his
> name John.**

This angel told Zacharias about the future and
also told him what God's will was. He told him,
"Make sure you call the boy's name John, not
Zacharias!" (As a side note, we ought to pray about
what we are going to name our children instead of
just picking a name because it sounds good.)

Let's continue reading in Luke chapter 1 about
the message the angel delivered to Zacharias.

> **LUKE 1:14-18
> 14 And thou shalt have joy and gladness; and
> many shall rejoice at his birth.**

15 For he shall be great in the sight of the Lord, and shall drink neither wine nor strong drink [Here we see an angel giving instructions on how to rear the child!]; **and he shall be filled with the Holy Ghost, even from his mother's womb.**
16 And many of the children of Israel shall he turn to the Lord their God.
17 And he shall go before him in the spirit and power of Elias, to turn the hearts of the fathers to the children, and the disobedient to the wisdom of the just; to make ready a people prepared for the Lord.
18 And Zacharias said unto the angel, WHEREBY SHALL I KNOW THIS? for I am an old man, and my wife well stricken in years.

In verse 18, Zacharias asks the angel, "How can I really know this is true?" Here Zacharias has an angel standing in front of him, whose very appearance was such that it made him tremble in fear. Then this revelation or word from God comes forth, and Zacharias forgets all about the appearance of the angel. He asks, "Now how do I really know this? I'm an old man, and my wife is old too." He's asking for a sign. The angel himself was a sign!

Notice the angel's remark. *"...I am Gabriel, that stand in the presence of God; and am sent to speak unto thee, and to shew thee these glad tidings"* (v. 19). This verse says that the angel came from the throne of God — from God's Presence — to deliver the message to Zacharias.

That means that Zacharias was not believing what God was saying to him through the angel! Yes, the message was delivered by the angel, but the message came from God. So it was no longer a matter of Zacharias' not believing what the *angel* had said, but a matter of his not believing what *God* had said!

The next verse shows us the consequence of Zacharias' unbelief and his provocation of the angel of God.

> **LUKE 1:20**
> **20 And, behold, thou shalt be dumb, and not able to speak, until the day that these things shall be performed, BECAUSE THOU BELIEVEST NOT MY WORDS, which shall be fulfilled in their season.**

Zacharias provoked the angel that was sent to him. And in provoking that angel, he got his mouth silenced! Zacharias couldn't speak another word until after his son John was born!

When the time came for his son to be born, people asked Zacharias, "What shall we call his name?" As they were discussing calling him something else, Zacharias wrote them a note, saying, "His name is John." Suddenly, Zacharias' tongue was loosed and he could speak again!

Zacharias learned his lesson the hard way, and I want to point out that it was his words that got him into trouble. The ministry of John the Baptist was very important, because he was to be the forerunner to Jesus. Because this was a highly important birth, there could be no mess-ups. Zacharias provoked the angel, and look what happened as a result.

I hope you can see the importance your words have on whether you benefit from the ministry of angels or from *any* blessing God has provided. God's Word spoken from your lips will not return to Him void or without producing results. One reason for that is that angels are hearkening to that Word, too, and they will minister to you accordingly.

So I encourage you to activate the ministry of angels on your behalf by speaking words that are in line with the Bible!

Chapter 3

The Integral Role Of Angels in Our Lives

We've been studying God's Word to see how angels are involved in the lives of His people — heirs of salvation. I said that there are ten areas in which angels are involved in people's lives, and one of those areas is healing.

> **JOHN 5:1-4**
> 1 After this there was a feast of the Jews; and Jesus went up to Jerusalem.
> 2 Now there is at Jerusalem by the sheep [market] a pool, which is called in the Hebrew tongue Bethesda, having five porches.
> 3 In these lay a great multitude of impotent folk, of blind, halt, withered, waiting for the moving of the water [Why would they do that?].
> 4 FOR AN ANGEL went down at a certain season into the pool, and troubled the water: whosoever then first after the troubling of the water stepped in was made whole of whatsoever disease he had.

God can use angels to minister healing to His people. You see, angels were created by God to serve Him. God then determined that He wanted angels to serve His people too. Angels were created to be servants for God, but when God had children, He wanted His servants to take care of His kids too!

You see, God is not selfish. He shares everything He has with His children. He hasn't held anything back from us — including the ministry of angels!

You Must Believe Before You Can Benefit From the Ministry of Angels

So in this passage in John chapter 5, we see an angel involved in healing. Thank God for angels — they are God's servants for us! Whenever we thank God for something, we should also thank Him for our angel. And every morning when we get up, we should say to our angel, "You were sent to minister for me. I am an heir of God, so get about the business that God intended for you. Protect me. Bring me words from God. Do everything God sent you to do, because I believe in your ministry."

When you believe in the ministry of angels, that's when the ministry is free to operate in your life. Just as with anything else in God's Word, it's when you believe that you receive that you will have what you are believing for (Mark 11:24).

Of course, a person can't believe in something he doesn't know about. Romans 10:17 says that faith comes by hearing, and hearing by the Word of God. The Bible also says, "How shall they hear without a preacher?" (Rom. 10:14). So if no one preaches on a particular subject to you, you won't have faith to believe it, which means you won't receive the full benefits of it. That is why I'm teaching on the subject of angels — so you'll get the full benefit of their important ministry!

Angels Can Protect You From Harm and Even Death

Angels are not weak servants. Remember, we said that angels excel in strength. They can do all sorts of things — I listed ten ways they are involved in our day-to-day lives.

There are things which have happened in your life that you don't understand how in the world you came through. I want you to know that an angel was involved in those situations! You may be alive today because an angel saved your life.

In my own case, I almost died three different times in my life. One incident should have certainly killed me, and I can tell you that there is no natural explanation for why I'm still alive today.

Years ago, I fell asleep at the wheel of my car while driving on a certain stretch of highway. Back in those days, I was going to college at Eastern Michigan University, and I traveled that particular highway from Detroit every single day. So I knew that road like the back of my hand. I knew every bend and every turn.

At the time of this particular incident, I had been out very late at night for several nights straight, and I was trying to get to one of those 7:00 a.m. classes. As I was driving, I was fighting to stay awake. I had the windows rolled down and the music turned up! I did everything I could think of to keep from falling asleep at the wheel.

I was going at least seventy miles per hour (back then, that was the speed limit). I fell asleep at the wheel, and when I woke up, I was miles down the road on a different stretch of highway! To get to where I was on that highway, I had to have taken a huge turn, and I did it while I was asleep!

When I woke up with my head leaning on the driver's-side window, I was driving in my lane of traffic — as if I had been awake the entire time! In my sleep, I had made that huge turn, even driving around a concrete wall. There was no way I could have gone around it without steering my car around it. The road was not straight!

It was as if someone else was driving my car that morning. And I know who it was. It was an angel of God! An angel was protecting my life, making sure that I did not smack into that concrete pillar at seventy miles per hour and wake up in Heaven with my work already finished!

You may have had circumstances in your own life in which you were spared. It was the ministry of an angel that spared you! Remember, angels are God's servants *for* you. They excel in strength, and they can protect you!

Angels Can Deliver
Very Important Instructions

We already saw in the case of Zacharias, father of John the Baptist, that angels can be involved in giving revelation and delivering messages from God. Now we're going to look at another instance in which an angel delivered very important instructions to Joseph, who was engaged to be married to Mary.

In Matthew chapter 1, we find that Mary is great with child. Mary and Joseph had not yet married, and, of course, Joseph had not had sex with her. So when Mary became pregnant, Joseph knew that someone else must have done the deed, so to speak. But Joseph was a good man, so he

wasn't going to make a big scene about it. He was
just going to put her away privately.

> **MATTHEW 1:20,21**
> **20 But while he thought on these things, behold,
> the ANGEL OF THE LORD appeared unto him in a
> dream, saying, Joseph, thou son of David, fear not
> to take unto thee Mary thy wife: for that which is
> conceived in her is of the Holy Ghost.**
> **21 And she shall bring forth a son, and thou shalt
> call his name Jesus [Savior]: for he shall save his
> people from their sins.**

In this instance, Joseph obeyed the instructions
of the angel who appeared to him. Joseph didn't
say, "What are you talking about? What do you
mean? I've never heard of anything like this
before." No, Joseph just obeyed the word from God
that was delivered by the angel. He didn't speak
contrary to the word from God, and it came to pass
just as the angel had told him.

We must remember that corrupt communication binds our angels. You see, man's word is his
will toward God. And God's Word is His will toward
man. In the Bible, we see angels who were very
much involved in the lives of people. We also see
that the ministry of angels was affected by the
words those people spoke.

Angels Can Reveal
The Plan and Purpose of God

The Apostle John is another Bible example of someone who received revelation from God through an angel. John received this revelation, which we call the Book of Revelation, during his exile on the Isle of Patmos.

Let's begin with Revelation 22:7.

REVELATION 22:7-9
7 Behold, I [Jesus] come quickly: blessed is he that keepeth the sayings of the prophecy of this book.
8 And I John saw these things, and heard them. And when I had heard and seen, I fell down to worship before the feet of the ANGEL which shewed me these things.
9 Then saith he unto me, See thou do it not: for I am thy fellowservant, and of thy brethren the prophets, and of them which keep the sayings of this book: worship God.

Notice in verse 8, John didn't fall down to worship Jesus. Jesus wasn't the one who showed him those things. It says it was an *angel* who revealed them to John. And it says that John fell down at the feet of the one who gave him the revelation.

Again, who gave him the revelation? The angel did. The entire Book of Revelation — all the wondrous things in Revelation — was revealed to John by an angel.

Notice something else in verse 9. The angel said, "Don't bow down to worship me, because I'm your fellowservant." The angel was telling John, "I'm your servant. And I'm the servant of your brethren, the prophets, and of them which keep the sayings of this book."

The same angel who revealed the Book of Revelation to John was also the servant of the prophets and of others who obeyed God's Word. Angels are servants of *anyone* who will obey what the Word says! Angels are *your* servants if you obey the Word. When you speak the Word, angels work for *you*!

Angels Can Serve Us Even After Death

Let's look at a familiar passage of Scripture to see yet another way angels can serve us.

> LUKE 16:19-22
> 19 There was a certain rich man, which was clothed in purple and fine linen, and fared sumptuously every day [He must have been rich if he wore the best clothes every day!]:
> 20 And there was a certain beggar named Lazarus, which was laid at his gate, full of sores,

**21 And desiring to be fed with the crumbs which
fell from the rich man's table: moreover the dogs
came and licked his sores.
22 And it came to pass, that the beggar died, and
was carried by the angels into Abraham's bosom. . . .**

Abraham's Bosom was the place where Old Testament saints — those who were believers — went
when they died physically. Today we know that
Abraham's Bosom has been emptied out. But at
the time when this event in Luke chapter 16 took
place, Old Testament saints couldn't go to Heaven,
because Jesus hadn't come yet; therefore, they
weren't born again.

So Old Testament saints waited in Paradise or
Abraham's Bosom until Jesus carried out God's
plan of redemption. The Bible says that when
Jesus had done that, He carried captivity captive
(Eph. 4:8).

In other words, when Jesus came out of hell —
having defeated the devil, making a show of him
openly and triumphing over him in the Cross (Col.
2:15) — He stopped by Abraham's Bosom and
declared to all the Old Testament saints, "I am the
King of kings and Lord of lords! I'm the One you
taught and prophesied about. I'm the One you
didn't get to see. Believe in Me!" They did, and
they were taken to Heaven.

But I want you to notice from this passage in Luke 16 that after Lazarus had died, the angels carried him to the place of the saints. In the *Living Letters,* one verse in First Corinthians 15 says, "Death is your servant to bring you to Christ." You see, even in the death of a saint, an angel is still serving him by taking him to Heaven.

I've been ministering to people for more than twenty-five years. Throughout my years of ministry, I've made many hospital visits and have had to deal with many people who were sick. I've seen many of them healed and some who were not. But over the years, I've heard some of the people I was visiting tell me that they saw their angel. The day they saw their angel was usually the day before they went home to be with the Lord. Sometimes it was the very day they went home, and sometimes it was as much as a week before they went home.

In every case, when the person saw an angel, he would report that the angel was just standing in the corner, waiting. You see, God's angels are the ones who handle the death of the saints, bringing them up into Heaven and leading them through the Gate of Glory!

Now I want you to know that angels are not only strong, but they're also beautiful. And angels hang around the very throne of God. If one of your friends or relatives who knew Jesus has died and has gone home to Heaven, don't you feel sorry for him. I'm telling you, the moment he stepped out of that earthly body, an angel of God took him by the hand. Your loved one probably looked up and said, "Oh, how *beautiful!*" And then that angel ushered him to the very throne of God in glory!

Christians need to understand that angels are involved in handling death. The Bible says, *"Precious in the sight of the Lord is the death of his saints"* (Ps. 116:15). In fact, it's so precious that He sends a "welcome party" from Heaven! An angel of God is with us from the time we are born until the time we die, and then that angel even takes us into glory. Thank God for the ministry of angels! Angels are God's servants for us!

Angels Can Deliver Us From Even Hopeless Situations

Let's continue our study of angels' involvement in the everyday lives of God's people.

ACTS 12:1-5
1 Now about that time Herod the king stretched forth his hands to vex certain of the church.

2 And he killed James the brother of John with the sword.
3 And because he saw it pleased the Jews, he proceeded further to take Peter also. (Then were the days of unleavened bread.)
4 And when he had apprehended him, he put him in prison, and delivered him to four quaternions of soldiers to keep him; intending after Easter to bring him forth to the people.
5 Peter therefore was kept in prison: but PRAYER was made without ceasing of the church unto God for him.

There is a reference in my Bible for the word "prayer" in verse 5, which says, "Instant and earnest prayer." This tells us that the prayer the Church made unto God on Peter's behalf wasn't some sloppy prayer. They didn't pray, "Well, Lord, help him. You know everything, Lord. Don't let him die."

No, the kind of prayer they made is called supplication. Supplication is done with emotion at times. This earnest prayer of supplication was being made without ceasing unto God on Peter's behalf.

ACTS 12:6,7
6 And when Herod would have brought him forth, the same night Peter was sleeping between two soldiers, bound with two chains: and the keepers before the door kept the prison.
7 And, behold, the angel of the Lord came upon him, and a light shined in the prison: and he smote Peter on the side, and raised him up, say-

**ing, Arise up quickly. And his chains fell off from
his hands.**

This incident with Peter took place in the Age
of Grace, which is the same age we live in — also
known as the Church Age. One thing that means
is, the same things that happened in the Book of
Acts are still available for the Church today! The
Book of Acts is not the "Acts of the Apostles."
That's the wrong name for it, because, really, it's
the acts of the *Holy Spirit*! And as Christians
today, we are still living in the age of the Holy
Spirit. That means His acts are still available for
us today!

We see in Acts 12:7 that when the angel of the
Lord came to Peter, a light shone in the prison.
The angel smacked Peter on the side, so to speak,
and picked him up, saying, "Get up, quick!" When
the angel did this, the chains fell off Peter's hands.

Notice that this angel was involved in the
deliverance of Peter, a man of God, from death at
the hands of a man filled with demon spirits.
Angels are involved in delivering and protecting
God's people!

The angel said to Peter, "Get up and put on
your sandals." Now Peter could have told the angel,

"No, I'm not going with you." But he didn't. Peter obeyed the words of the angel.

I think if *I* knew I were going to die within twenty-four hours, I would have gone with the angel too! And that's what Peter did. He got up, put on his shoes, and went with the angel.

> **ACTS 12:9-11**
> **9 And he** [Peter] **went out, and followed him** [the angel]**; and wist not that it was true which was done by the angel; but thought he saw a vision.**
> **10 When they were past the first and the second ward, they came unto the iron gate that leadeth unto the city; which opened to them of his own accord: and they went out, and passed on through one street; and forthwith the angel departed from him.**
> **11 And when Peter was come to himself, he said, Now I know of a surety, that the Lord hath sent his angel, and hath delivered me out of the hand of Herod, and from all the expectation of the people of the Jews.**

In verse 10, we learn that Peter thought he was seeing a vision. But it was no vision. That angel was real! That angel was manifested to Peter "in the flesh"!

After they left the prison, Peter and the angel went up to a big iron gate, which was so heavy, apparently, that men had to pull it open. But it says the gate opened "of his own accord." (Remember, they didn't have remote-controlled gates back then like we do now. Now we just press a button and the gate opens!)

Notice the angel was personally involved in delivering Peter. The angel got rid of Peter's chains, opened the gate, and took him to a place of deliverance. Only then did the angel leave.

Prayer Activates the Forces of God

Why did this supernatural occurrence happen? It happened because people *prayed*. Prayer is the key to activating all the forces of God. Any kind of revival in the Church, even a restoration of all that God has for the Church, starts with the Church's being involved with prayer.

Every Christian ought to have a prayer life. When a believer prays in other tongues, he is praying the perfect will of God (1 Cor. 14:2). When a Christian is praying in other tongues, he may be directing an angel to bring deliverance to him and open the gate in his life that's been holding him back!

ACTS 12:12-16
12 And when he [Peter] had considered the thing, he came to the house of Mary the mother of

> John, whose surname was Mark; where many
> were gathered together praying.
> 13 And as Peter knocked at the door of the gate, a
> damsel came to hearken, named Rhoda.
> 14 And when she knew Peter's voice, she opened
> not the gate for gladness, but ran in, and told how
> Peter stood before the gate.
> 15 And they said unto her, Thou art mad. But she
> constantly affirmed that it was even so. Then said
> they, It is his angel.
> 16 But Peter continued knocking: and when they
> had opened the door, and saw him, they were
> astonished.

In this passage of Scripture, we find Peter
delivered from prison and going to Mary's house.
He knocks on the door, and a woman named Rhoda
looks out, sees that it's Peter, and gets so happy
that she forgets to open the door. Instead, she runs
to the back of the house where the saints are praying, and she says, "It's Peter!"

They answered her, "No, it's not Peter. Peter's in
prison. He needs to be delivered. That's why we're
praying for him!"

I know that probably sounds comical, but, in
effect, that is what they were saying. Actually, they
said to her, "...*Thou art mad* [or, "You're crazy."]...."
Even when Rhoda insisted that it was Peter and
they found Peter at the door, they said, "It must be
his angel"!

You see, these saints were so use to having interaction with angels that they more readily believed that the man Rhoda had seen was an angel than they believed it was Peter!

Suppose a person you know was taken down to the county jail unjustly. And although he was charged with a serious crime, you know he didn't do it. So your entire church starts praying. And while you're at someone's house praying, there's a knock on the door. Someone looks out through the peephole and sees the person you're busy praying for — the one who's been locked up in jail for a crime he didn't commit.

Then imagine that the person looking through the peephole becomes so filled with joy that he runs to where everyone is praying and says, "Hey, he's out there on the porch!"

Do you think that the group praying would say, "That isn't him — that's his angel"? No, they probably wouldn't say that.

But, you see, these men and women in the Book of Acts were familiar with the operation of angels. They had experience with angels. They had seen angels, and they understood that every believer had one. So the group of people praying in Acts chapter 12 said, "No, it's not Peter. It's his angel."

Of course, verse 16 tells us that the knocking continued, so they opened the door. Peter came in, and everyone was shocked. But the point I want to make is, firstly, an angel was involved in delivering Peter.

Secondly, I want you to notice the familiarity with angels that the saints had. We have come a long way from that kind of familiarity. But those same angels are still here in the earth and still assigned to minister to the saints. The Church needs to have a revelation of the fact that there are angels here to assist us!

I want to show you something else regarding angels in connection with Peter's escaping from prison.

> **ACTS 12:19-23**
> **19 And when Herod had sought for him [Peter], and found him not, he examined the keepers, and commanded that they should be put to death. And he went down from Judaea to Caesarea, and there abode.**
> **20 And Herod was highly displeased with them of Tyre and Sidon: but they came with one accord to him, and, having made Blastus the king's chamberlain their friend, desired peace; because their country was nourished by the king's country.**

> 21 And upon a set day Herod, arrayed in royal apparel, sat upon his throne, and made an oration unto them.
>
> 22 And the people gave a shout, saying, It is the voice of a god, and not of a man.
>
> 23 And immediately the ANGEL OF THE LORD smote him, because he gave not God the glory: and he was eaten of worms, and gave up the ghost.

Herod was highly displeased with the keepers of Peter, because when they went into that prison, where Peter was being held for the Gospel's sake, they couldn't find him. They didn't know what happened, because an angel had gone in and released Peter. Herod was displeased and had Peter's keepers executed as a result.

Now Herod was a powerful king, and people revered him. Verse 22 says, *"And the people gave a shout, saying, It* [Herod's voice] *is the voice of a god, and not of a man."*

Now look at verse 23: *"And immediately the ANGEL OF THE LORD smote him* [Herod], *because he gave not God the glory: and he was eaten of worms, and gave up the ghost."*

I told you, those angels are bad boys! And I'm telling you now that God is their Creator.

God was the Creator of angels. And Satan, or Lucifer, was the most beautiful of them (*see* Ezekiel 28:11-19). He was the most glorious. But God found something in him that caused him to be expelled from Heaven.

What did God find? *Pride.* Lucifer got lifted up in pride because of all his attributes. So he lost his position and got thrown down to the earth. And, remember, I said that those fallen angels will receive no mercy, grace, or forgiveness, because God does not look at angels the way He looks at man.

There is mercy, grace, and forgiveness for us, because we are precious to God, and He is mindful of us. And He has given us His angels as our servants to minister for us whatever it is we need — healing, protection, revelation, or deliverance!

Thank God for the ministry of angels! Now I realize this teaching about angels may sound "heavy" to you, but I encourage you to study the ministry of angels to God's people in the Bible. Study God's Word along this line until you become conscious of the ministry of angels and keenly aware that angels are here to assist, aid, and help *you*.

Chapter 4

Angels Are Our 'Power Tools'!

God gave us angels so that we would understand that He has put tools in the earth for us to use. Most of the time, we think of angels in regard to Heaven, but He put angels right here on earth — in our house, in our car — wherever we go!

God wants us to understand that there is someone standing right by our side who is exceedingly strong! Our angel is stronger than the most powerful munitions our Armed Forces can muster. You could shoot an angel with a high-powered rifle, but it wouldn't harm him. Instead, that angel would probably just take the gun and break it in half! Angels are strong, and, as our servants, they have the ability to strengthen us.

In Luke 22, we find an example of angels at work strengthening Someone — Jesus Himself — as He prayed in the Garden of Gethsemane.

> **LUKE 22:39-43**
> **39 And he came out, and went, as he was wont, to the mount of Olives; and his disciples also followed him.**

40 And when he was at the place, he said unto them, Pray that ye enter not into temptation.
41 And he was withdrawn from them about a stone's cast, and kneeled down, and prayed,
42 Saying, Father, if thou be willing, remove this cup from me: nevertheless not my will, but thine, be done.
43 And there appeared an ANGEL unto him from heaven, STRENGTHENING him.

The Greek word translated "strengthening" in verse 43 means *invigorating*. Jesus needed to be invigorated. There He was in that garden, knowing He was going to die on the Cross and that doing so was going to be the toughest thing He would ever have to do. His flesh didn't want to do it, so He knelt down and began to pray. And as He was praying, an angel came and strengthened Him.

God intends for angels to be involved in the day-to-day life of the believer in *this* day and age. It's not just the people in the Bible God was concerned about. He wants us to benefit from the ministry of angels *today*.

Rev. Kenneth E. Hagin has seen angels many times. One time, the Lord even showed Brother Hagin his own angel. And, recently, a certain minister was preaching at the church I pastor, and he had an encounter with an angel. He said God showed him an angel and told him it was an angel of prosperity. Well, we know that angels are involved in every area of the lives of the saints. They do their bidding according to the Word of God. In other words, what God's Word says, angels *do*!

In the twenty-five years that I've been preaching, I've had many people at different times tell me that they've seen angels during my services. Some have reported that when the anointing would come on me in a service, they'd see an angel approach me and speak to me, and, as he did, I would take off running across the platform!

You see, angels handle the anointing too. And they've been sent forth from God to strengthen us. Jesus is Lord, but Jesus also has a Body. We, the Church, are the Body of Christ. And the Bible says that we are heirs of God and joint-heirs with Jesus (Rom. 8:17). So since Jesus received an angel to strengthen Him when He prayed in the Garden of Gethsemane, guess what *we* can expect? An angel can strengthen us too!

Angels Can Equip Us
To Do God's Will With Power!

God sends forth angels to invigorate us when we pray so that we can do the will of God. When Jesus walked out of that garden after being strengthened

by the angel, He completed the will of God with
power! And I'm not talking about just a little bit of
power! For example, when the soldiers who were
looking to arrest Jesus walked up to Him and said,
"We're looking for Jesus," Jesus simply said, "I am
He," and they all fell backward to the ground (John
18:4-6)!

An angel will invigorate you in the same way —
by strengthening you and enabling you to complete
the will of God with power!

God has sent you an angel that is exceedingly
strong. That angel excels in strength, and He will
hearken unto the voice of the Word of God to
strengthen *you*!

Angels Can Strengthen You To Receive From God What He Wants To Give You

There is yet another Bible example of someone's
being strengthened by an angel. In the following
passage, we see Daniel seeking the will of God for
the future — for the children of Israel's destiny.

DANIEL 10:1-3
1 In the third year of Cyrus king of Persia a thing
was revealed unto Daniel, whose name was called
Belteshazzar; and the thing was true, but the time
appointed was long: and he understood the
thing, and had understanding of the vision.

2 In those days I Daniel was mourning three full weeks.

3 I ate no pleasant bread, neither came flesh nor wine in my mouth, neither did I anoint myself at all, till three whole weeks were fulfilled.

Now Daniel was interested in the future of Israel and in the plan and purpose of God for that great nation. It says Daniel went on a three-week fast and sought the Lord.

Now when the Word says that Daniel didn't eat any "pleasant bread," it doesn't mean that he didn't eat anything at all. It means that he didn't eat the kinds of things that he would normally eat. In other words, he cut down on the amount he was eating, and he just ate what was just absolutely necessary as he sought God's face for weeks.

Some Christians today get upset when they seek God for a couple of hours and don't seem to get any response. They start saying, "Well, God isn't hearing me. This 'seeking the Lord' business doesn't work."

That kind of talk is foolishness. Actually, it's corrupt communication. Sometimes it takes more than just a couple of hours to seek the Lord.

DANIEL 10:5
5 Then I [Daniel] **lifted up mine eyes, and looked, and behold A CERTAIN MAN** [an angel] **clothed in linen, whose loins were girded with fine gold of Uphaz.**

Notice the clothes on this "guy." The suit he's wearing is gold. But it's not just gold — it's *fine* gold. This angel who appears to Daniel is wearing a real gold suit, not a *gold-colored* suit!

Angels aren't paupers! They stand in the very Presence of God, and those whom God has appointed to watch after you are "decked out" from head to toe! The angels are dressed like that, and they are your servants. So since *they're* decked out, what do you think God wants for *you*?

How stupid can we be to think that it's the will of God for us to be poor, broke, sad, mad, and discouraged. It isn't the will of God for us to be poor if our servants are dressed in real gold! Are the servants greater than the master? I think not!

DANIEL 10:6
6 His [the "certain" man Daniel is talking about] **body also was like the beryl, and his face as the appearance of lightning, and his eyes as lamps of fire, and his arms and his feet like in colour to**

**polished brass, and the voice of his words like
the voice of a multitude.**

It's important to understand the terminology
that Daniel used to describe the angel's appearance. He could only describe the angel using the
language of his day.

Daniel saw something extraordinary. The angel
was extraordinarily dressed, and he was extraordinary in his appearance. So in verse 6, Daniel says,
*"His body also was like the beryl, and his face was
as the appearance of lightning, and his eyes as
lamps of fire, and his arms and his feet like in
colour to polished brass, and the voice of his words
like the voice of a multitude."*

Verse 7 of Daniel chapter 10 goes on to explain
what happened to the men around Daniel when
the angel appeared.

DANIEL 10:7
**7 And I Daniel alone saw the vision: for the men
that were with me saw not the vision; but A
GREAT QUAKING FELL UPON THEM, so that
they fled to hide themselves.**

Sometimes in meetings, we see people begin to
shake. I'll tell you what that is: It's the power of
God coming upon them! Now I'm not talking about
the flaky stuff that some people do. I grew up in a

Pentecostal denomination, and sometimes I saw people doing all kinds of quaking and shaking that wasn't caused by God at all.

In our day, the genuine "quaking and shaking" under the power of God first started at the Azusa Street Revival when the Holy Ghost moved in such a powerful way that these things began to take place. But sometimes the genuine move of God can get taken to extremes.

Let me give you a little history of the Azusa Street Revival. At the time William Seymour was filled with the Holy Ghost and started speaking with other tongues, the whole planet didn't believe that the baptism in the Holy Ghost or speaking in other tongues was for today. In fact, very few believed in it!

That's how far the Church had gotten away from the Book of Acts. But at the turn of the century in Los Angeles, California, on Azusa Street, revival took place. The Assemblies of God denomination, the Church of God in Christ, and the entire modern Pentecostal movement was born out of that mighty move of God.

Incidentally, that's when the term "holy rollers" came into existence. Men and women of God began to be called holy rollers because they were operating so much under the anointing that it would cause their bodies to quake and shake!

So when I talk about shaking under the influence of the power of God, I'm not talking about a "put on," when a person isn't really under the anointing at all. No, I'm talking about the real thing. There are times when the anointing comes on people, and they will genuinely begin to quake and shake. Ushers don't need to "catch" them; the anointing is on them! In fact, whoever grabs them to try to catch them might catch some of the same anointing!

The Day of Pentecost is coming back to the Church! In the Book of Acts where it talks about believers coming out of that Upper Room filled with the Holy Ghost, they were actually drunk in the Spirit! That great move of the Holy Ghost is being restored to the Church!

Let's continue reading in Daniel chapter 10.

DANIEL 10:8-12
8 Therefore I was left alone, and saw this great vision, and there remained no strength in me: for my comeliness was turned in me into corruption, and I retained no strength.
9 Yet heard I the voice of his words: and when I heard the voice of his words, then was I in a deep sleep on my face, and my face toward the ground.

> 10 And, behold, an hand touched me [notice the
> angel touched him], which set me upon my knees
> and upon the palms of my hands.
> 11 And he said unto me, O Daniel, a man greatly
> beloved, understand the words that I speak unto
> thee, and stand upright: for unto thee am I now
> sent. And when he had spoken this word unto me,
> I stood trembling.
> 12 Then said he unto me, Fear not, Daniel: for
> from the first day that thou didst set thine heart
> to understand, and to chasten thyself before thy
> God, thy words were heard, and I am come for thy
> words.

Notice what the angel said to Daniel in verse
12: "The very first day you prayed, God heard your
words and started answering." God sent an angel
to Daniel simply because of the words that were
coming out of Daniel's mouth for the three weeks
as he was fasting and praying.

Prayer Enacts the Covenant
And Seals the Future

I know what Daniel must have been saying to
God. You see, Daniel had a covenant with God, and
he was probably talking about that covenant, saying, "I have a right to speak over the children of
Israel! I have a right to pray about their future! I
have a right to see them blessed!" He probably

remembered the words in Isaiah, where God said, "Come before Me and plead your case" (Isa. 43:26).

Remember, the angel told Daniel, "I am come because of your words." (Remember that angels come and go because of our words.)

> **DANIEL 10:13,14**
> **13 But the prince of the kingdom of Persia withstood me one and twenty days** [three weeks]: **but, lo, Michael** [we all know Michael is an angel], **one of the chief princes, came to help me; and I remained there with the kings of Persia.**
> **14 Now I am come to make thee understand what shall befall thy people in the latter days: FOR YET THE VISION IS FOR MANY DAYS.**

The vision Daniel had as he sought the Lord did come to pass, but not until many, many years later. It actually began to come to pass when the children of Israel reestablished the nation of Israel in 1948! At that time, the Hebrew people from all over the known world began to travel back to the Promised Land. That migration marked the beginning of the last days that we are living in.

> **DANIEL 10:15-19**
> **15 And when he had spoken such words unto me, I set my face toward the ground, and I became dumb.**
> **16 And, behold, one like the similitude of the sons of men touched my lips: then I opened my mouth,**

and spake, and said unto him that stood before me, O my lord, by the vision my sorrows are turned upon me, and I have retained no strength.

17 For how can the servant of this my lord talk with this my lord? for as for me, straightway there remained no strength in me, neither is there breath left in me.

18 Then there came again and touched me one like the appearance of a man, and he strengthened me,

19 And said, O man greatly beloved, fear not: peace be unto thee, be strong, yea, be strong. And when he had spoken unto me, I was strengthened, and said, Let my lord speak; for thou hast strengthened me.

Daniel said in verse 16 that the angel looked like a man. He didn't say that he *was* a man, but that he had the similitude of a man. In other words, Daniel was saying, "He looked like a man, but I knew he wasn't one."

Angels Can Take Your Breath Away — And Give It Back to You Again!

Then Daniel begins to describe what happened next, saying, "The angel touched my lips. Then I opened my mouth and said, 'By the vision, my sorrows are turned upon me, and I have no strength. And how can you speak a mes-

sage to me, seeing as I have no breath in me'"
(vv. 16,17).

Now look again at verse 18.

> **DANIEL 10:18**
> **18 Then there came again and touched me one
> like the appearance of a man, and he STRENGTH-
> ENED me.**

When Daniel told the angel, "I don't have any
strength to stand before you," the angel strengthened him just as he would strengthen Jesus later
in the Garden of Gethsemane. We know the angel
invigorated Daniel, because verse 19 says,
"... [the angel] *said, O man greatly beloved, fear
not: peace be unto thee, be strong, yea, be strong.
And when he* [the angel] *had spoken unto me, I*
[Daniel] *was strengthened, and said, Let my lord
speak; FOR THOU HAST STRENGTHENED
ME.*"

Notice the change in Daniel! Now he says, "Go
ahead and talk to me, because I am strengthened!" For a moment, he was saying, "I don't
have the strength for all this." Remember, he had
been fasting for three weeks. His body was tired.
But that angel touched Daniel and strengthened

him. Then the angel spoke to him and strengthened him some more.

After the second strengthening, Daniel said to
the angel, "Now tell me what you have to tell me.
I'm ready."

So the angel relayed the message as recorded in
Daniel 10:20 and 21. It is this passage that further
reveals the identity of the extraordinary speaker.
Here we learn that he is indeed an angel.

> **DANIEL 10:20,21**
> **20 Then said he** [the angel]**, Knowest thou where-
> fore I come unto thee? and now will I return to
> fight with the prince of Persia** [a demon spirit]**: and
> when I am gone forth, lo, the prince of Grecia
> shall come.**
> **21 But I will shew thee that which is noted in the
> scripture of truth: and there is none that holdeth
> with me in these things, but Michael your prince.**

In these verses, the speaker is telling Daniel, "I
am a prince too." An angel is often referred to as a
prince. Therefore, we can know that it was an
angel who revealed unto Daniel what would happen in the last days! It was an angel from God
Almighty who was sent to strengthen Daniel and
answer him the moment he prayed!

Chapter 5

Angels: The Prayer And Praise Connection

In the last chapter, we read that God sent angels to answer Daniel the minute he prayed. And those same angels are here in the earth right now, answering the moment *we* pray!

However, it's important to remember that there was a "time lag" between the time Daniel prayed and the time he got the revelation. You see, there is warfare going on in this earth's atmosphere. But just as Daniel's angel won, yours will win too!

The angel sent from God will always win when there is a believer who is standing in faith and not getting over into doubt — speaking in fear, depression, despondency, and all that garbage. As we said before, angels hearken unto the voice of the Word!

When a Christian is standing on the Word of God, he is allowing his angels to do their job. And those angels will be involved in answering his prayer and strengthening him to make it all the way to the end of his journey! No wonder the Bible says, "Let the weak say, 'I am strong'" (Joel 3:10)!

Angles Are Encamped Round About Us

So far in our study of angels, God's servants for us, we have seen angels involved in strengthening. We've seen angels involved in healing. We've seen angels involved in deliverance. We've seen angels giving revelation. We've seen angels doing battle. We've seen angels helping at the time of death. We've seen angels involved in protecting people. We've seen angels looking like men. We've seen angels delivering messages and giving direction concerning the future.

Now there's something else we need to see that the angels do. It's found in Psalm chapter 34. And what we are about to read is what the angels are still doing right now — in this day and age!

> **PSALM 34:1,2,7**
> **1 I will bless the Lord at all times: his praise shall continually be in my mouth.**
> **2 My soul shall make her boast in the Lord: the humble shall hear thereof, and be glad....**
> **7 The angel of the Lord encampeth round about them that fear him, and delivereth them.**

First, let's look at verse 2: *"My soul shall make her boast in the Lord...."* How do we make our boast in the Lord? With our mouth!

With my mouth I boast in God! With my mouth I say that all my needs are supplied according to God's riches in glory (Phil. 4:19)! I say that all of my bills are paid! I say that everyone in my house will be saved and filled with the Holy Ghost! I say that God will give me the best job I ever had! I say that every sickness and every disease that comes against my body dies in the Name of Jesus, for I am His temple, and the God I serve is stronger than anything that could ever come against Him.

That is how you boast in the Lord!

Notice David said, "I boast in my God." He was saying this very thing when he was in that cave with four hundred of the most scared and sorry bunch of men in the whole country (1 Samuel 22:2)! Despite his predicament, David made his boast in God.

David said, "I will bless the Lord at all times. I will not do anything but praise God. I will praise Him when circumstances look good, and I will praise God when they don't look so good!

We need to have that same attitude. We need to say, "I'm going to praise God when I feel like it and praise Him when I don't! I'm going to praise God when I go to work and praise God if I have no work to go to! I'm going to praise God when my family does right and praise God if they don't do right! I'm

going to praise God regardless of what any man
says. And I'm going to boast in my God at all times,
because I know my God makes a way even when
there *is* no way!"

PSALM 34:3-8
3 O magnify the Lord with me, and let us exalt his
name together.
4 I sought the Lord, and he heard me, and delivered
me from all my fears.
5 They looked unto him, and were lightened: and
their faces were not ashamed.
6 This poor man cried, and the Lord heard him, and
saved him out of all his troubles.
7 The angel of the Lord encampeth round about
them that fear him, and delivereth them.
8 O taste and see that the Lord is good: blessed is
the man that trusteth in him.

Verse 3 says, "O, magnify the Lord with me!" In
other words, David was saying, "I don't want to do
this by myself. I want my brothers and sisters to
come on and help me praise God. Let's magnify
God together! Let's give Him praise together! Let's
lift up His Name together! Let's shout the victory
before Him together!"

This passage goes on to say, *"I sought the Lord,
and he heard me, and delivered me from all my
fears. They looked unto him, and were lightened:
and their faces were not ashamed. This poor man*

cried, and the Lord heard him, and saved him out of all his troubles. The angel of the Lord ENCAMPETH ROUND ABOUT THEM THAT FEAR HIM, and delivereth them" (vv. 4-7).

Notice it didn't say that the angels encampeth round about *him* — it said the angels encampeth round *them. Them who?* Them that praise God! Them that boast in the Lord! Them that magnify God! Them that seek the face of God! The angels of God get around all them that fear Him, and the angels deliver them!

Sometimes when I'm preaching in one of my churches on this subject, and I want to give the congregation an idea of what it means to have angels encamped round about them, I have the men and women on my church staff come to the platform and form a circle around me. Now I am pretty tall, so some of the people on staff are shorter than I am. Yet even though they aren't as tall as I am, when they all gather around me, the congregation can hardly see me!

Angels Excel in Strength *and* in Size!

When Brother Hagin saw his angel, he said the angel was at least nine feet tall. That means that the men and women who form a circle around me are really short compared to the angels! I am nowhere near nine feet tall, so if the congregation can't see me when the *staff members* get around me, then when I praise God and *angels* encircle me — the devil can't see me for all the angels!

The Bible says that the angels of God encamp round about them that worship God. Angels surround us when we praise God! That's why the devil doesn't want us to praise the Lord. That's why he doesn't want us to worship God. That's why he doesn't want us to testify and confess the Word, because when we do these things, we loose the angels of God to work on our behalf!

Angels strengthen us! They work for us! They bring money to us! Angels aid in our healing and in our deliverance! And the angels of God are available to the Church *right now*. Thank God for the ministry of angels!

Your Devotion to God Can Activate Angels

Remember the story of Daniel and the lions' den in Daniel chapter 6? He had been told, "You cannot pray to any other god besides the king for thirty days. If you do, you will be thrown into the den of lions. You must do what the king has decreed!"

But Daniel refused. He still got up every morning and prayed to the God of Israel! He wasn't going to worship any idol god. He was going to praise only *his* God, the true and living God! So the rulers took Daniel and threw him into the lions' den! They said that he would be gone — eaten — by morning!

But the next day the king went down to the lions' den, and he saw Daniel sleeping on the head of a lion! He yelled down into the den, "Oh, Daniel, has the Lord delivered you?"

Daniel replied, *"My God hath sent his ANGEL, and hath shut the lions' mouths, that they have not hurt me: forasmuch as before him innocency was found in me; and also before thee, O king, have I done no hurt"* (Dan. 6:22).

The Lord sent His angel, and His angel stopped the mouth of the lions! And you need to believe God has sent *you* an angel that will help you in your time of need.

And your angel is a big boy! He's dressed in fine clothes, and he is exceedingly strong! His job is to work for you. He's just waiting for instructions! It's time for you to open your mouth and say, "Lord, I praise and magnify You today. I know that whatever comes my way is not bigger than You! I know that everything is going to all right!

"In the Name of Jesus, I say that all of my bills are paid! In the Name of Jesus, I say my body is healed! In the Name of Jesus, I say my cupboards are filled! In the Name of Jesus, I have a way made for me! Now, angel, you go do what I say! Bring me my job! Bring me my money. Bring me my spouse! Bring back my wayward child!"

We Are Not Alone!

God wants us to remember that there are angels all around us. We are not alone! We are not weak and defenseless — God has sent us help! Standing right by our side is an angel of God! And he looks good! If someone comes against us and tries to take us out of here, if we will praise God and say, "I'm not afraid, for God has not given me the spirit of fear, but of power and of love and of a sound mind" [2 Timothy 1:7], the angel will step in and move back the danger!

The angel of God has saved my life many times! And the angel of God will save *your* life! Angels will watch your home! And angels will watch your car! It's time to believe what God has said about the ministry of angels.

Pray, Praise, and Receive

Someone may ask, "Bishop, what do I have to do so I can benefit from the ministry of angels?" *Get your words in line with God's Word!* Start believing God! And, most of all, *pray!* Pray and praise! Pray and make your request known to God (Phil. 4:6). Then praise Him because you believe that you receive. Remember, God is good all the time! And He's on your side!

Bless the Lord at *all* times! When you get up in the morning — when you're still wiping the sleep from your eyes — bless the Lord! When your boss says you're fired, bless the Lord! When someone doesn't want to have anything to do with you, bless the Lord! When your kids act crazy, bless the Lord! Bless the Lord at *all* times! Make your boast in the Lord, and let His praise continually be in your mouth!

It doesn't matter what the situation looks like, with God, we know what the outcome is going to be! We know that we win! We know that the angels are working for us, and if we need it, they will give us a word from the Lord! An angel will speak in our ear and say, "Go here and see this person" or "Go there and see that person." If we make the turns our angel tells us to make, he'll make sure the people we need to see are where they're supposed to be!

Notice one more thing in Psalm chapter 34. After the Psalmist David spoke about the angel, he said, *"O taste and see that the Lord is good: blessed is the man that trusteth in him. O fear the Lord, ye his saints: for there is no want to them that fear him. The young lions do lack, and suffer hunger: but they that seek the Lord shall not want* [lack] *any good thing"* (vv. 8-10).

In other words, if we seek the Lord, we won't lack any good thing. Why? Because angels are encamped all around us. They go when we say go, and they cause the money we need to come to us!

Put Action to Your Faith

Now it's time for you to put your faith into action. How do you act on what you've learned? Just lift your hands right now and say, "In the Name of Jesus, I thank You, Father God, for the ministry of angels. In Jesus' Name, I believe what Your Word says about the ministry of angels.

"I thank You, Lord, that they are sent for me to help me! I am an heir of salvation! Angels, in Jesus' Name, I say that I am blessed! I say I am healed! I say I have favor! I say ways of deliverance are made for me — every time I need them — in the Name of Jesus! I say I have abundance and no lack! I say the Lord brings me out of trouble, difficulty, and bondage — every time!

"Angels, in Jesus' Name, go produce my words! Go do what I just said! Cause the circumstances to turn in my favor! Now, Father God, I'm going to do what David did! I'm going to bless You with my mouth! I'm going to boast in You with my mouth! I'm going to magnify You with my mouth!"

It's no wonder we can say, "God is good all the time!" We can say, "all the time," because there's an angel with us *all the time*! So when the devil says, "I'm going to knock you out," you can tell him, "Go see 'my boy'! He'll take care of you!"

A Word From the Lord

And now you will say,

"I know the Lord has sent an angel my way.

And now because I know these things,

I will act and sing, and my praises will ring.

I'll go before God with a hop in my step,

And I'll laugh and rejoice no matter what comes against me to try and stop me in the middle of my way.

I know that God is on my side,

And there is nothing the enemy can do.

For an angel of God is there to see me through and through.

So, rejoice, O people, and give Him praise and glory,

Because God has provided for what you need in this time of glory!

Yes, it's the Age when things are being restored.

And even the ministry of angels shall once again come to the fore!"

Chapter 6

Angels Can Help You Enter Your 'Promised Land'

We know that angels are ministering spirits sent to minister *for* us. But did you know that when you were born, an angel was assigned to you?

MATTHEW 18:10
10 Take heed that ye despise not one of these little ones; for I say unto you, That in heaven their angels do always behold the face of my Father which is in heaven.

Why are these children's angels beholding the face of the Father? To get instructions as to what to do for the children!

As I said, when you were born, there was an angel assigned to you (an angel is assigned to every baby when he is born). And just because you grow up does not mean that your angel leaves you!

But whether or not your angel is allowed or permitted to do for you what God intends for that angel to do — to assist, aid, and help you — is up to what you do (or what your parents do when you

are a child). It depends on whether or not you follow God and speak His Word.

As we said, angels can assist us in a number of
ways. They can help us enter into and receive
everything that God has for us — our "promised
land," so to speak.

Let's look at Exodus chapter 23 about the
instructions God gave Moses concerning the children of Israel before they were to enter into their
Promised Land.

EXODUS 23:17-20
**17 Three times in the year all thy males shall
appear before the Lord God.**
**18 Thou shalt not offer the blood of my sacrifice
with leavened bread; neither shall the fat of my
sacrifice remain until the morning.**
**19 The first of the firstfruits of thy land thou shalt
bring into the house of the Lord thy God. Thou
shalt not seethe a kid in his mother's milk.**
**20 Behold, I send an ANGEL before thee, to keep
thee in the way, and to bring thee into the place
which I have prepared.**

Now the children of Israel were about to go into
their Promise Land, the land God had sworn to
Abraham to give to His people. Of course, we know
that the Promised Land was occupied; it was
already inhabited. Other nations were there, but

God had said, "This is your land. It belongs to you. However, in order to get the land, the current inhabitants are going to have to be driven out."

So Moses gave the children of Israel certain requirements that they were going to have to follow now that they had escaped Egypt and were headed for this Promise Land.

Notice Exodus 23:20: *"Behold, I send an Angel before thee, to keep thee in the way, and to bring thee into the place which I have prepared."*

Another way to say that is, "I'm sending an angel in front of you to cover the front side." In other words, the angel was going to take the point! And just what was that angel going to do at the point?

EXODUS 23:20
20 Behold, I send an Angel before thee, **TO KEEP THEE** in the way, and **TO BRING THEE into** the place which I have prepared.

Now the Lord said two things: *First*, He said, "I'm going to send an angel. The angel is going to go in front of you." *Second*, God said, "The angel is going to take care of you while you're on your journey. That angel is going to be the one that's going to bring you into what My will is for you."

God's will for the children of Israel was that they inhabit the Promise Land. But notice what He used to get them where they needed to be. He had an angel involved in leading them there.

But that's not all. Look at verse 21.

EXODUS 23:21
21 Beware of him, and obey his voice, provoke him not; for he will not pardon your transgressions: for my name is in him.

Who is the Lord talking about when He said, "Beware of him"? *The angel that God was sending before them!* It was the angel that was going to be with them as they journeyed and that would bring them into the place God had for them.

I talked about this briefly in another chapter, but verse 21 just told us again that an angel can be provoked and that *if we provoke him, there are consequences.* Well, one way to provoke an angel is by going against what God has said. For example, if the Lord says, "You *can,*" and you say you *can't,* you will provoke God and the angel He sent to help you. Remember, we said that corrupt communication will hinder or bind the ministry of angels on your behalf.

Let's continue reading in Exodus 23.

EXODUS 23:23
23 For mine ANGEL shall go before thee, and bring thee in unto the Amorites, and the Hittites, and the Perizzites, and the Canaanites, the Hivites, and the Jebusites: and I will cut them off.

Now we get an understanding of how God did what He did. *He did it through the ministry of angels!*

When the children of Israel went into the Promised Land as recorded in the Book of Joshua, they went up against the very first nation or group of people they had to drive out, and it was Jericho. Jericho was surrounded by a wall so wide that six chariots could race side by side on top of that wall!

God told Joshua, "I want you to march around that wall once every day. And on that last day, the seventh day, I want you to march around it seven times and then blow the trumpet. And those walls will fall down flat" (Joshua 6:3-5).

But how was it that the walls fell down flat? When the people obeyed God and did what He said to do, guess who knocked that wall down? The angel that took them into the land to drive out the Amorites, Hittites, and all the other "-ites" who were there! That land didn't belong to those "-ites," and

God sent an angel to fight the battle for the children of Israel!

The Bible tells us that those who were under the Old Covenant don't have a better covenant than we do under the New Covenant! Whatever they had in the Old Covenant, we have in the New Covenant, plus more (Heb. 8:6). And the angels that fought those battles for God's people in the Old Covenant and knocked down walls will fight battles and knock down walls in our covenant too!

Angels Can Help Us Retrieve Stolen Property

Remember, God had said, "I'll send that angel to go in front of you. I'll send that angel to be with you. And I'll send that angel to take you into the place that's prepared for you, and He will fight for you"!

Angels were involved in helping the children of Israel get back what the devil had stolen from them. And they will do the same for us today!

Let's keep reading in Exodus 23.

EXODUS 23:24-26
24 Thou shalt not bow down to their gods, nor serve them, nor do after their works: but thou

Angels Can Help You Enter Your 'Promised Land'   89

shalt utterly overthrow them, and quite break
down their images.
25 And ye shall serve the Lord your God, and he
shall bless thy bread, and thy water; and I will
take sickness away from the midst of thee.
26 There shall nothing cast their young, nor be
barren, in thy land: the number of thy days I will
fulfil.

I tell you, I like that phrase in verse 26: "...*nor
be barren....*" In other words, God was saying that
there will be no setbacks in childbirth!

Then God said, "...*the number of thy days I will
fulfil*" (v. 26). That's talking about health and healing, praise God! That's talking about blessing! God
was saying, in essence, "Whatever you touch will
be blessed, because I'm going to drive out all the
inhabitants, and I'm going to use My angels to
clear the way for you."

Now the Church of the Lord Jesus Christ has
largely not benefited in recent times from the ministry of angels, because we have let the truth about
angels slip. We let it "leak out," so to speak. If
we're not believing God or speaking His Word concerning a certain subject in the Bible, we're not
going to reap the benefits of it. But we can change
that! All it takes is some knowledge.

Let's look at Joshua chapter 7 and learn a very important lesson about relying on God and the ministry of angels instead of upon our own strength and power.

JOSHUA 7:2-5
2 And Joshua sent men from Jericho to Ai, which is beside Bethaven, on the east side of Bethel, and spake unto them, saying, Go up and view the country. And the men went up and viewed Ai.
3 And they returned to Joshua, and said unto him, Let not all the people go up; but let about two or three thousand men go up and smite Ai; and make not all the people to labour thither; for they are but few.
4 So there went up thither of the people about three thousand men: and they fled before the men of Ai.
5 And the men of Ai smote of them about thirty and six men: for they chased them from before the gate even unto Shebarim, and smote them in the going down: wherefore the hearts of the people melted, and became as water.

When the children of Israel had gone into the Promised Land and starting defeating all those different nations, it was an angel every time who did the fighting and brought the victory. It was an angel who brought the wall down at Jericho, knocking it flat.

Sin Will Short-Circuit
The Ministry of Angels

Then the very next place they went after that was Ai. By the time the children of Israel got to Ai, they were so cocky because they'd had such a great victory at Jericho that they said, "We don't need the whole army. Just send a few men down there, and they'll 'mop up' Ai. After all, it's a much smaller nation. They don't have the same kind of defenses that Jericho had. Just send a few men down there to take it."

But when they went down there, they got run off instead! Their soldiers were killed. Joshua went to God and said, "God, what happened? We won the battle at Jericho, but we lost at Ai!"

And God said, "Get up and shut up. There's sin in the camp."

Someone asked, "Bishop Butler, do you mean that sin can stop angels from performing?"

Yes, that's exactly what I mean! You see, God is against sin for one reason, and it's not because God is against fun. No, God is against sin *because He loves you*! He is against sin, because sin will kill you! And sin will stop the angels from going before you, clearing the way and bringing you into God's best for your life.

Sin can have an element of fun to it — the Bible calls it the pleasure of sin for a season (Heb. 11:25). But Romans 6:23 says, *"...the wages of sin is death...."* That's talking about death and all its various manifestations. In other words, sin will make you poverty-stricken. It will make you diseased. It will cause family break-ups.

That's why you can't afford to live in sin. You can't afford not to follow God. When you follow God, you get blessed by God. When you follow God, you get God's protection and things work out for you. It's as simple as that.

Now let's look at Acts chapter 7 at another account of Moses' and the children of Israel's exodus out of Egypt and their possessing the Promised Land. The discourse is given through Stephen, the first deacon in the Church.

To give you some background, a deacon was a servant; he was not a ruler. The deacon's job was to wait on tables. In other words, he ministered to or waited on people. Yet we read that there were some big-time qualifications for that position. Deacons had to be men of faith and filled with the Holy Ghost — in order to wait on tables (Acts 6:3)!

Well, guess what? An usher today, then, ought to be filled with faith and the Holy Ghost. And a parking-lot attendant ought to be filled with faith and the Holy Ghost. And, *certainly*, a nursery worker ought to be filled with faith and the Holy Ghost. *Anything you do for God, you ought to be filled with faith and the Holy Ghost to do it!*

Stephen, of course, was doing deacon work, but he was also out there laying hands on people and getting them healed. Miracles were happening in his ministry.

Just because miracles happen when you lay hands on people doesn't mean you're called to a pulpit ministry or a fivefold ministry. *Every* child of God is supposed to walk in the supernatural. For example, it says in Mark 16:18, *"...they* [believers] *shall lay hands on the sick, and they shall recover."*

Some folks pray and have something happen, and they think, *Oh, I must be called to preach!* But God didn't necessarily call them. And if He didn't call them, all they're going to do is make a mess of things because they're intruding into an area where God has not called them.

Angels Are 'Flames of Fire'

Well, our man Stephen's out there preaching, and certain people are really mad at him because he's causing such a raucous. So the

Sanhedrin nabs him, but Stephen just starts preaching to his captors, talking about Moses and the children of Israel and *angels*!

ACTS 7:23-30

23 And when he [Moses] **was full forty years old, it came into his heart to visit his brethren the children of Israel.**

24 And seeing one of them suffer wrong, he defended him, and avenged him that was oppressed, and smote the Egyptian:

25 For he supposed his brethren would have understood how that God by his hand would deliver them: but they understood not.

26 And the next day he shewed himself unto them as they strove, and would have set them at one again, saying, Sirs, ye are brethren; why do ye wrong one to another?

27 But he that did his neighbour wrong thrust him away, saying, Who made thee a ruler and a judge over us?

28 Wilt thou kill me, as thou diddest the Egyptian yesterday?

29 Then fled Moses at this saying, and was a stranger in the land of Madian, where he begat two sons.

30 And when forty years were expired, there appeared to him in the wilderness of mount Sina an ANGEL OF THE LORD in A FLAME OF FIRE in a bush.

What was Stephen talking about in verse 30 when he said, *"...an angel of the Lord..."*? Stephen was talking about what Moses saw — "an angel of the Lord in a flame of fire in a bush" (v. 30).

Moses was in the backside of the desert being a shepherd. He had left Egypt at forty years of age because he counted it better to be with the children of God than to live in sin for a season as a son of Pharaoh. So Moses was out there shepherding, and, one day, he saw a burning bush. The bush was burning, yet it was not consumed (Exod. 3:2).

(What Moses actually saw and what Hollywood depicts that he saw are not the same. The movies depict fire, and it may have *looked* like fire. But, actually, it was not fire Moses saw; it was an angel of the Lord.)

When Moses looked at that bush at what looked like fire to him, he was seeing one of God's angels who *appeared* as a flame of fire. When Moses saw it, he wondered at the sight, and, as he drew near to behold it, the voice of the Lord came unto him. And, of course, that was when the Lord told him, "I've called you to go back to Egypt to get My people. You're going to be their deliverer" (Exod. 3:7-10).

Let's continue reading Stephen's discourse.

ACTS 7:35
35 This Moses whom they refused, saying, Who made thee a ruler and a judge? the same did God send to be a ruler and a deliverer by the hand of the ANGEL which appeared to him in the bush.

In other words, God sent Moses to Egypt to get the children of Israel out of Egypt. And He sent Aaron with Moses. But guess what else God sent to get the job done? *An angel.* It was an angel that brought the wrath upon Pharaoh and Egypt. It was an angel that caused all those plagues to assail the Egyptians. It was an angel that delivered the children of Israel when Pharaoh's army came against them.

I tell you, angels are *bad*! Angels are *tough*! And you'd better not mess with them!

Remember, Hebrews 2:3 says, *"How shall we escape, if we neglect so great salvation...."* And Hebrews 1:14 says, *"Are they not all ministering spirits, sent forth to minister for them who shall be heirs of salvation?"* Well, since the angel of God could bring about such a great salvation and get the children of Israel out of Egypt, he can surely get you out of your neighborhood if you need to get out! Glory to God!

Let's continue reading what Stephen had to say in Acts chapter 7.

> **ACTS 7:36-38**
> **36 He brought them out, after that he had shewed wonders and signs in the land of Egypt, and in the Red sea, and in the wilderness forty years.**
> **37 This is that Moses, which said unto the children of Israel, A prophet shall the Lord your God raise up unto you of your brethren, like unto me; him shall ye hear.**
> **38 This is he, that was in the church in the wilderness with the ANGEL which spake to him in the mount Sina, and with our fathers: who received the lively oracles to give unto us.**

Remember, God's people were getting ready to go into the Promise Land. They'd been delivered from Egypt and then had spent forty years in the wilderness. And even while they were in the wilderness, they were taken care of by an angel of the Lord.

> **ACTS 7:38,39**
> **38 This is he [Moses], that was in the church in the wilderness with the angel which spake to him in the mount Sina, and with our fathers: who received the lively oracles to give unto us:**
> **39 To whom our fathers would not obey, but thrust him from them, and in their hearts turned back again into Egypt.**

I encourage you to read the entire passage in Acts chapter 7, all the way down to verse 53.

> **ACTS 7:51-53**
> **51 Ye stiffnecked and uncircumcised in heart and ears** [this is Stephen talking to the religious leaders], **ye do always resist the Holy Ghost: as your fathers did, so do ye.**
> **52 Which of the prophets have not your fathers persecuted? and they have slain them which shewed before of the coming of the Just One; of whom ye have been now the betrayers and murderers:**
> **53 Who have received the law by the disposition of ANGELS, and have not kept it.**

Who gave Moses the Law? It came from the mouth of an angel. God had an angel in that bush; God had an angel go with Moses to Egypt; God had an angel get His people out of Egypt; God had an angel "handle" Pharaoh's army; God had an angel protect His people in the wilderness; God had an angel speak to Moses the Law which was written down for the children of Israel to follow; and God had an angel take them into the Promise Land.

So, you see, there is a ministry of angels, and God uses it for His people!

When you know how to benefit from the ministry of angels that God has provided, there isn't an Egypt you can't escape, a "Red Sea" you can't cross, or a wilderness you can't be protected in! And there's not a word from God you can't receive because God will get His provision to you through the ministry of an angel!

Chapter 7

'So Much Better'

We've covered in-depth from both the Old Testament and the New Testament the ministry of angels in the day-to-day lives of believers. But there's more concerning the ministry of angels!

In Daniel chapter 6, we read about and touched on briefly the fact it took the ministry of angels to rescue Daniel from the lions' den. An angel protected and delivered him from a den of hungry lions because Daniel knew how to activate the ministry of angels on his behalf.

To give you a little bit of background, everyone knew that Daniel was a man of God, and certain men were jealous of him. So they went to the king and persuaded him to sign a decree saying that no one could pray to any other god but the king for thirty days.

Do you know what Daniel did? Daniel prayed before God three times a day, as was his custom, giving thanks unto his God. His attitude was, *I don't care what they say. My God is God. I'm going to pray to Him, and that's all there is to it! They can take my life, but it doesn't matter. I'm going to worship God!*

I want you to know that God appreciates that kind of attitude.

Let's pick up reading in verse 16.

> **DANIEL 6:16**
> **16 Then the king commanded, and they brought Daniel, and cast him into the den of lions. Now the king spake and said unto Daniel, Thy God whom thou servest continually, he will deliver thee.**

You see, the king was sorry about the law that he'd decreed, because he favored Daniel. He was the one who'd appointed Daniel as prime minister in the first place. When the king signed the decree into law, he didn't realize that he was being manipulated by Daniel's enemies.

But even the king could not change a decree of the Medes and the Persians. Once he signed it, he must carry it out. He was obligated to enforce it.

So the king was forced to throw Daniel into the den of lions. But this king had faith in God. He said to Daniel, "Your God will deliver you from the lions." (Now when even the unbeliever knows to

believe God, *we* certainly ought to be believing
Him!)

> DANIEL 6:17-22
>
> 17 And a stone was brought, and laid upon the
> mouth of the den; and the king sealed it with his
> own signet, and with the signet of his lords; that
> the purpose might not be changed concerning
> Daniel.
>
> 18 Then the king went to his palace, and passed
> the night fasting: neither were instruments of
> musick brought before him: and his sleep went
> from him.
>
> 19 Then the king arose very early in the morning,
> and went in haste unto the den of lions.
>
> 20 And when he came to the den, he cried with a
> lamentable voice unto Daniel: and the king spake
> and said to Daniel, O Daniel, servant of the living
> God, is thy God, whom thou servest continually,
> able to deliver thee from the lions?
>
> 21 Then said Daniel unto the king, O king, live for
> ever.
>
> 22 My God hath sent his ANGEL, and hath shut
> the lions' mouths, that they have not hurt me:
> forasmuch as before him innocency was found in
> me; and also before thee, O king, have I done no
> hurt.

One angel took on all those lions! What happened was, Daniel was thrown into the lions' den,
and those lions said, "Yum! Dinner!"

But God had other plans, and He used the ministry of angels to carry them out and to rescue His man, Daniel!

Someone said, "Yes, but those lions had probably already been fed, so they weren't very hungry. *That's* why Daniel was not hurt."

But the Bible tells us in verse 23 why Daniel was not hurt. It says, *"...So Daniel was taken up out of the den, and no manner of hurt was found upon him, BECAUSE HE BELIEVED IN HIS GOD."*

> **DANIEL 6:24**
> 24 And the king commanded, and they brought those men which had accused Daniel, and they cast them into the den of lions, them, their children, and their wives; and the lions had the mastery of them, and brake all their bones in pieces or ever they came at the bottom of the den.

Those lions were hungry, all right! I mean, according to this verse, when the king had Daniel's accusers thrown in, before their bodies hit the floor, those lions grabbed them in mid-air and tore them to shreds!

If those lions could have talked, when Daniel was thrown in, they would probably have said, "Dinner is served!" But Daniel knelt before his God and said, "I believe in Your deliverance." And an angel showed up and began slapping those lions 'upside the head' as they came forth to eat. I mean, there was a whole lot of whipping going on!

Then the angel said to one of the lions, "You lie there," and Daniel lay down on its mane!

I want you to know that if an angel of God can take on all those lions, he can surely take on those folks at your job who are giving you a hard time! And he can surely take on all the other people who come against you!

Our Better Covenant
Includes the Ministry of Angels

God has deliverance for you, friend. It's in the hand of an angel! *"Are they not all ministering spirits, sent forth to minister FOR them WHO SHALL BE HEIRS OF SALVATION?"* (Heb. 1:14). That's talking about us!

HEBREWS 1:1-4
1 God, who at sundry times and in divers manners spake in time past unto the fathers by the prophets,
2 Hath in these last days spoken unto us by his Son, whom he hath appointed heir of all things, by whom also he made the worlds.
3 Who being the brightness of his glory, and the express image of his person, and upholding all

things by the word of his power, when he had by
himself purged our sins, sat down on the right
hand of the Majesty on high;
4 Being made SO MUCH BETTER than the angels,
as he hath by inheritance obtained a more excellent name than they.

Notice that phrase, "so much better." This is
what the Book of Hebrews is about. You'll find in
Hebrews that Jesus is so much better than the
angels. He's so much better than Moses. He's so
much better than anything else that could come
along. He's not just better; He's *so much better*!

Because of Jesus, we have a better covenant
established upon better promises (Heb. 8:6). And
our "so-much-better" covenant includes the ministry of angels!

By now, I hope you noticed that when God said,
"I'm going to do such-and-such" or "I'm going to protect the children of Israel," He meant, "I'm going to
send My angels to do it. Angels have been the ones
involved in deliverance for centuries and centuries.

Yet God made Jesus to be so much better than
the angels.

HEBREWS 1:4
4 Being made so much better than the angels, as
he hath by inheritance obtained a more excellent

name than they [than Michael and all the other angels].

Jesus' Name is more excellent than Gabriel. Jesus' Name is more excellent than the highest-ranked angel.

> **HEBREWS 1:5**
> **5 For unto which of the angels said he at any time, Thou art my Son, this day have I begotten thee** [today you are born of Me]**? And again, I will be to him a Father, and he shall be to me a Son?**

Notice the last part of that verse: *"...And AGAIN, I will be to him a Father, and he shall be to me a Son?"* That means there was a time when Jesus was the Son of God and then, for a moment in time, ceased to be. When was that? When He was made to be sin on the Cross (2 Cor. 5:21). Remember, Jesus said, "My God, why have You forsaken Me?" (Matt. 27:46; Mark 15:34).

Everything God Has Done, He Did for Us

Why did God forsake Jesus for that brief moment? Why did He let that happen? *For me and for you.* The only time Jesus the Son was separated from the Father was on our behalf. But, praise

God, because Jesus was obedient unto death (Phil. 2:8), God said, *"...AGAIN, I will be to him a Father, and he shall be to me a Son."*

> **HEBREWS 1:6-8**
> 6 And again, when he bringeth in the firstbegotten into the world, he saith, And let all the angels of God worship him.
> 7 And of the angels he saith, Who maketh his angels spirits, and his ministers a flame of fire.
> 8 But unto the Son he saith, Thy throne, O God, is for ever and ever: a SCEPTRE OF RIGHTEOUSNESS is the sceptre of thy kingdom.

Do you know what a scepter is? It was the possession of kings. It was something they used that signified their royalty. A scepter was usually gold, encased with diamonds and other precious stones. And if the king put his scepter out to you, you could approach him. But if he *didn't* extend his sceptre, you *couldn't* approach him.

Well, verse 8 said, "Righteousness is the scepter of Your Kingdom." In other words, we are in right-standing with God through our faith in Jesus Christ. And, through His righteousness, we can approach the throne of grace! Through His righteousness, we can appropriate everything that God has provided for us, including the ministry of angels!

The Bible says that we are seated with Christ in heavenly places (Eph. 2:6). Well, it says that Jesus is at the right hand of the throne of God (Eph. 1:20). But the angels of God (as bad or tough as they are!) cannot get to that position. Yet God gave it to us!

Let's keep reading in Hebrews chapter 1.

HEBREWS 1:9-14
9 Thou [Jesus] hast loved righteousness, and hated iniquity; therefore God, even thy God, hath anointed thee with the oil of gladness above thy fellows.
10 And, Thou, Lord, in the beginning hast laid the foundation of the earth; and the heavens are the works of thine hands:
11 They shall perish; but thou remainest; and they all shall wax old as doth a garment;
12 And as a vesture shalt thou fold them up, and they shall be changed: but thou art the same, and thy years shall not fail.
13 But to which of the angels said he at any time, Sit on my right hand, until I make thine enemies thy footstool?
14 Are they not all ministering spirits, sent forth to minister for them who shall be heirs of salvation?

Look at verse 9: *"Thou hast loved righteousness, and hated iniquity; therefore God, even thy God, hath anointed thee with the oil of gladness above thy fellows."* The "oil of gladness" is talking about the Holy Spirit. He is the oil of *gladness*, not the oil of *sadness*! Churches where everyone is sad, mad, and discouraged, saying, "Woe is me — nobody knows the trouble I've seen" don't have a flow of Holy Ghost!

Where there's a flow of the Holy Ghost, there's gladness; there's jumping, running, shouting, singing, and dancing! Why? Because the Holy Ghost is the oil of gladness!

Now notice verse 13: *"But to which of the angels said he at any time, Sit on my right hand, until I make thine enemies thy footstool?"* God didn't say that to any one of the angels — as bad as they are! No, He said that to Jesus, because Jesus is so much better!

God's Best Belongs to 'Someone Else'

Then verse 14 says that angels are ministering spirits sent forth. This is talking about the same angels who were rejected from sitting at the right hand of the throne of God where Jesus sits. In other words, they didn't get what He got, because He is so much better. Those angels were rejected so that a place could be made for *someone else* to be seated with Jesus at God's right hand. I'm going to show you who that "someone else" is.

Remember it says, *"But unto the Son he saith, Thy throne, O God, is for ever and ever..."* (Heb. 1:8). And in Hebrews 1:6 it says, *"And again, when he bringeth in the FIRSTBEGOTTEN into the world, he saith, And let all the angels of God worship him."*

We Are Born of God!

God said to Jesus, "You're the first-begotten into the world." Well, if there's a first-begotten, which means *first-born*, then there's at least a second-born, because God is talking about sons here. And we know that not only is there a second-born, but there's a third-born, a fourth-born, and so forth. Because of Jesus the first-born, we can be called sons of God (John 1:12). I don't know what number-born I am, but I'm one of those born!

We are that "someone else" whom God made to be seated with Christ in heavenly places!

Friend, we can't neglect the ministry of angels, because angels are God's servants for us. We are His sons and daughters, and He has provided for us the ministry of angels.

HEBREWS 2:1,2
1 Therefore we ought to give the more earnest heed to the things which we have heard, lest at any time we should let them slip.

**2 For if the word spoken by angels was stedfast,
and every transgression and disobedience received
a just recompence of reward.**

Look at verse 2: *"For if the word spoken by angels was
stedfast...."* We saw that when God's angels said something, that's exactly what happened, because *"...every
transgression and disobedience received a just recompense of reward."* Just ask the king (Herod) who was
stricken down and turned to worms about this verse!

Then it says, *"How shall we escape, if we neglect
so great salvation; which at the first began to be spoken by the Lord, and was confirmed unto us by them
that heard him"* (v. 3). Why does this verse use the
phrase "so great salvation"? Because angels are
great deliverers!

I realize this subject of angels may seem a little
abstract for some people, because they can't see
angels with their natural eyes. But, remember, even
though we can't see the wind, we can sure see its
effects!

We need to get over into faith and begin to
believe God for everything He has for us — including the ministry of angels! Then even if we can't see
our angels, we will certainly be able to see the
effects of their ministry for us! Angels are God's
servants for us!

Book Titles By Word of Faith Publishing

Bishop Keith A. Butler

Angels: God's Servants for You	BK010
A Seed Will Meet Any Need	BK003
Hell: You Don't Want To Go There	BK005
How To Be Blessed By God	BK013
The Last Week of Jesus	BK020
Success Strategies From Heaven	BK001 (Harrison House, Inc.)
What On Earth Are We Here For?	BK002 (Harrison House, Inc.)

Min. Deborah L. Butler

Establishing Godly Relationships Through Marriage and Family	BK012

Rev. Keith A. Butler II

God's Plan for the Single Saint	BK006